The Early Church Today Series

ST. ANTHONY THE GREAT

LETTERS OF SAINT ANTHONY THE GREAT

THE EARLY CHURCH TODAY SERIES

Volume 2

The early leaders of the Church, tasked with shepherding Christ's flock, left us spiritual wealth that is too often neglected in modern times. The Early Church Today Series, published by the St. Mary & St. Moses Abbey Press, aims to help make that richness more accessible to readers, inviting them to see the applicability of the early Church to our walk with God today. By sharing practical selections from the writings of the early Church, aided by meaningful editorial supplements and revisions, each book will attempt to diminish impediments and bring to light what the Church has to offer.

Letters of Saint Anthony the Great

Copyright © 2023 Coptic Orthodox Diocese of the Southern U.S.A.

All rights reserved.

Designed & Published by:
St. Mary & St. Moses Abbey Press
101 S Vista Dr, Sandia, TX 78383
stmabbeypress.com

Translation from Arabic by St. Mary & St. Moses Abbey.

The Arabic text was taken from *Bostan Al-Rohban Al-Mowasah, Al-joz' Al-Awal* [The Expanded Paradise of the Monks, Part 1]. (Egypt: St. Macarius Monastery, 2006); and *Rawdat Al-Nofous Fi Rasa'il Al-Kidees Antonious* [The Paradise of Souls in the Letters of Saint Anthony]. (Egypt: St. Anthony Monastery, 1899). Both books were used for this translation, to obtain a more accurate English translation, though we relied mainly on the first one. The collector of the material of the latter book, the monk Andrawis of Saint Anthony Monastery, indicates that the text was taken from the oldest copy that was previously translated from Coptic.

Contents

THE FIRST LETTER	5
THE SECOND LETTER	13
THE THIRD LETTER	19
THE FOURTH LETTER	25
THE FIFTH LETTER	28
THE SIXTH LETTER	32
THE SEVENTH LETTER	43

THE FIRST LETTER

On Leaving the World for Monasticism: And it is of Three Orders

A Letter of Anthony the Solitary and Chief of Solitaries to the Brethren in Every Place

Before all else, I offer you, my beloved, peace in the Lord, praying for your salvation in the Lord.

1. As I see it, the souls, to whom the good news of the Spirit of God reached, of men and women, are of three orders [or callings]:

The first order are those who accepted, through the law of nature and liberty, which is created first in them, what reached them of the good news by the word of mouth. And they were not negligent but hastened, with the readiness of obedience, as our father Abraham was ready through the law of nature. For God spoke to him, saying, "Go out of your country, and from the sons of your race, and go into the country which I will show you,"[1] and do not be double-hearted. So Abraham made ready for this calling, and became an example for those who [desire to] commence. And until now this calling remains immovable to whoever wants to enter into this form [that is, the monastic way of life]. And if they do so, their hearts being ready to follow the Spirit of God, they with ease receive the promises. This is the characteristic of the first order.

The second order are those who hear the written law, which testifies to them of the judgment to come for sinners, and of the good promises to come for those pursuing goodness. And by these testimonies, written in the law, their intents are roused and they seek to enter into this calling. As David the prophet said, "The law of the Lord gives life to the souls,"[2] and he also said, "Your words give me light, and Your law teaches the babes."[3] And writings such as these are abundant.

The third order are those whose hearts are hard, who are addicted to committing sins, so the merciful God brings upon them hardships and afflictions, till their hidden parts [that is, their inner senses] and their intents are roused, out of the abundance of what comes upon them, so they feel regret, return, ready themselves and enter into this calling; and they repent with all their heart, and receive the promises like the first and second orders.

These are the three orders, by which souls are called,

---

1 Cf. Genesis 12:1.
2 Cf. Psalms 19:7.
3 Cf. Psalms 119:130.

The First Letter

that they may return to the Lord, till they attain to the grace of the calling of the Son of God.

2. And I say that all those who entered with all their hearts into one of these callings, [should] learn patience, until they are able to resist the enemy. Those, before all else, the Holy Spirit calls and facilitates all matters for them, to sweeten for them the entrance into repentance, and reveals to them its true ways, that they may repent with their spirits and bodies, and return to God the Creator. So He supports them with power, till they subdue the body and spirit, to purify both, [both] becoming heirs of eternal life.

As for the body, we weary it with much fasting, keeping vigils, struggling, and the rest of the services with which a man subdues his body. And in these, the spirit of repentance assists the man, comforts him, and teaches him not to turn back, nor become attached to anything of the matters of the world. As for the spirit, its eyes are opened too to the knowledge of true repentance, so that it may be purified with the body, and both may be one in purity, because this is the teaching of the Holy Spirit; because He advances before them [that is, He leads them] and purifies them, and blots out from them the [foreign] qualities which are mingled with the body, and transfers both of them to the first creation [that is, the first state] which was theirs before the transgression. And nothing remains in man of the matters of the enemy. And thereupon the body becomes a follower of the will of the mind which purifies it from its food, drink, sleep, and the rest of its behaviors, and continually learns from the Holy Spirit, as the Apostle says, "I discipline my body and bring it into subjection."[4]

3. And I know that in the body there are three motions:

The first motion is constant in the body, and has no authority to do anything without the will of the soul, but indicates its existence in the body through a [normal] motion which is not sinful.

The second motion drives the body towards sumptuous food and drinks, and the heat of the blood that is generated from the abundance of food stirs up warfare in the body, and inclines it toward evil lusts. Therefore, our Lord Christ—glory be to Him—warned His disciples, saying, "Take heed to yourselves, lest your hearts be weighed down with overindulgence and drunkenness."[5] And Paul the Apostle says, "Do not be drunk with wine, of which is dissipation."[6] It is necessary, then, for all who have put on the garb of monasticism—[or those who seek the attainment of the measure of chastity]—to say with St. Paul, "I discipline my body and bring it into subjection."[7]

The third motion comes from evil spirits, to turn back those desiring to enter through the door of chastity.

But if the soul is armed with continual patience and with the testimonies which are of the breaths of God [that is, the word of God], then the Holy Spirit guides the mind to the purification of both the soul and body of these three motions. So if the person were negligent concerning these

---

4   1 Corinthians 9:27.
5   Cf. Luke 21:34.
6   Cf. Ephesians 5:18.
7   1 Corinthians 9:27.

testimonies and teachings, which he heard, then the evil spirits would overpower him and defile his body, making him think about how help might come to him! If the soul returned and clung to the Spirit of salvation, then it would learn that patience for the sake of God is its rest and peace.

4. These words I have said to you, my beloved, for the sake of the agreement between the body and soul in repentance. So if the mind receives this grace, then he prays in the Holy Spirit, and begins casting out of the soul all the hardships which come upon it from the lusts of the heart. And the Holy Spirit, if He has communion with the mind, to help it keep the commandments which it learned, guides it to[8] uproot from the soul these passions which have mingled with the body, one by one. Likewise, the soul's own passions, which are present in it, the Spirit utterly uproots, from the top of the head to the sole of the feet: so He places a rule for the eyes, that they may look with uprightness and purity, that there may not be in them any guile; and the ears, that they may hear peaceably, not longing to hear gossip, nor about people's falls and weaknesses, rather are pleased to hear good things and about mercy [shown] to the whole creation. And the tongue, also, the Spirit teaches to speak with purity, to always utter what is good. For the soul expresses the sickness, which it contracted, through the tongue; therefore, it [i.e. the tongue] has contracted a great sickness by which the soul is hit also, as James the Apostle said, "Whoever says, 'I serve God', and he does not bridle his tongue, he deceives his

---

8 *Expanded Paradise* adds here: how to.

heart, and his service is useless."[9] And he says in another place, "The tongue is a little member, but it utters great swelling things, and defiles the body."[10] And such [words] are plenteous in the Holy Scriptures.

So if the mind is strengthened, by the power of the Spirit, it will be purified and will learn to discriminate the words uttered by the tongue, that there may be in them no carnal will[11], and by this the saying of Solomon the wise is fulfilled: "All the words I was given from God, have no perversity nor crookedness in them."[12] And he also says, "The tongue of the righteous heals the sicknesses."[13]

And the hands too have other motions, which sometimes follow the will of the soul[14], and this ought not be so, because the Spirit has prepared them to move with purity, and to be raised in prayer, and to be stretched out for acts of mercy and giving. And for what they offer of pure prayers, what is written is fulfilled in them: "Let the lifting up of my hands be as the evening offering."[15] And concerning their being stretched out for mercy and giving, it says, "The hands of the strong give abundantly."[16]

And the belly also, the Spirit purifies, so that it becomes restrained in its eating and drinking, as the Spirit

---

9   Cf. James 1:26.
10 Cf. James 3:5–6.
11 i.e. self-will.
12 Cf. Proverbs 8:8.
13 Cf. Proverbs 12:18.
14 Or: the passion of the soul.
15 Cf. Psalms 141:2.
16 Cf. Proverbs 10:4.

says through the tongue of David the prophet, "I have not eaten with the one who has a greedy eye and gluttonous heart."[17] For if much food and drinks and insatiability gain dominion over the belly, and the carnal soul draws it to that, then the power of the enemy mingles with this carnal soul. Those who seek chastity, the Spirit of God guides them to His upright ways, and chastity and uprightness of the body support them, and in them the saying of Paul the Apostle is fulfilled, "Whether you eat or drink, or whatever you do, do all to the glory of God."[18]

5. And if the three motions I have mentioned prevailed against the flesh, to make it turn aside from correction[19], the one who seeks salvation in truth would take them away from himself with ease and would cling to purity, because the Spirit has become his refuge, strengthening him and quenching in him all evils and uncleanness which are stirred up against him, as our teacher Paul the Apostle said, "Put to death your members which are on the earth: fornication, uncleanness, passion, evil desire,"[20] and what follows.

And the feet too, if they were not upright and did not walk carefully according to God's will with restraint, then the heart, which has become filled with grace, would restrain them and make them walk according to the will of the Holy Spirit, that they may serve in good matters, that the body may be perfect in all goodness, and may become under the authority of the Holy Spirit. I say that if the whole

---

17 Cf. Psalms 101:5.
18 1 Corinthians 10:31.
19 "Uprightness" in *Expanded Paradise*.
20 Colossians 3:5.

body were purified, then it would take on something of the spiritual body which is to rise in the resurrection of the righteous.

All these we have said on the passions of the soul which have mingled with the body, and they [i.e. the passions of the soul] move it [the body] to become inclined towards evil passions, for they have become active in all the members of the body. And as I have said, the soul too has other motions, which we desire to make known to you, and these are: pride, the various passions other than the passions of the body, reproaching people, anger, weakness of heart, lack of self-control, and the rest of the passions. So if the soul delivers itself to the Lord, with all its might, then the good God gives it true repentance, and reveals to it these passions, one by one, that it may turn away from them, and the stirrings of the enemy, through the temptations which are meant to prevent the soul from getting rid of these motions, will not prevail against it. So if the soul continues in patient endurance and listening well to the Holy Spirit who draws it to repentance, the merciful Creator will have pity on its toil and the labors of the body, which are: much fasting, many vigils, meditation on Holy Scriptures[21], unceasing prayer, and serving all people with a pure heart and a poor spirit. If [the soul] continues in all of these, the good Lord will look to it and deliver it from all temptations, and save it with His mercy, and have mercy upon it, because He is the lover of mankind, to whom is due praise and glory, with His good Father and the Holy Spirit, forever and ever. Amen.

---

21 Literally: the books of God.

THE SECOND LETTER

To His Children the Monks; On the Giving of the Law, and the Incarnation of God the Word; and in it He Urges Them to Keep the Commandments

1. Anthony writes to his children, beloved in the Lord, and offers them peace.

Beloved in the Lord, God has visited His creation not once only, but at all time since the beginning of the world to its end. So whoever seeks the Lord diligently and with love, and hears His teachings, will be with Him, and He will give him the grace of the Holy Spirit.

And since the rational natures, joined with bodies, have grown weak, changed because of the motions of the soul, and died, not being able to realize its first creation, but "became as a beast,"[22] "and served the creatures rather than the Creator,"[23] the Creator of all has visited, with the

---

22 Cf. Jude 10.
23 Cf. Romans 1:25.

power of His goodness, His creation, by His life-giving laws. And those who were worthy of this grace, and walked according to the laws implanted in them, with all their might and intent, and received the Spirit of adoption, and were taught by the Holy Spirit—those were able to worship God as is proper, according to the saying of Paul the Apostle: "And all these, having obtained a good testimony through faith, did not receive the promise, God having provided something better for us, that they should not be made perfect apart from us."[24]

2. And because of His great love, being the God of all, He desired to visit our weakness. So He raised up for us Moses the prophet, through whose hands He gave us the Law, and set for us the foundation of the true house, that is the one, rational Church, because His will is to restore the creation to its first estate. So Moses built the house and did not complete it, but he went away and left it. Then God raised up after him the company of the prophets, by this one Spirit, so they also built upon the foundation which Moses laid, and did not complete [it], but went away and left it.

And when our spiritual fathers saw that this sickness had no healing, they knew that no one of this creation was able to heal it, except the Only-begotten of the Father alone, who is the Image of His eternity, through whom the whole creation, which is after His pattern, was [made]. And they were assured that He is the Savior and the Physician. So they diligently enquired for our sakes, for we are their

---

24 Hebrews 11:39–40.

fellows in the membership, saying, "Is there no balm in Gilead, is there no physician there? Why then is there no recovery for the health of the daughter of my people?"[25] "We would have healed her, but she is not healed. Forsake her, and let us go away from her."[26]

But God the Word, through His unfathomable love, came to us, according to the saying of His pure prophets: "Son of man, take for yourself the appearance of one going into captivity."[27] And He is the One who is perfect, "who, being in the form of God, did not consider it robbery to be equal with God, but made Himself of no reputation, taking the form of a bondservant, and coming in the likeness of men ['yet without sin'[28]]. And being found in appearance as a man, He humbled Himself and became obedient to the point of death, even the death of the cross. Therefore God also has highly exalted Him and given Him the name which is above every name, that at the name of Jesus every knee should bow, of those in heaven, and of those on earth, and of those under the earth, and that every tongue should confess that Jesus Christ is Lord, to the glory of God the Father."[29]

So from now on, beloved, let these words be clear to you, that God the Father, in His goodness, did not have pity on His only-begotten Son, but delivered Him up[30] for

---

25 Jeremiah 8:22.
26 Cf. Jeremiah 51:9.
27 Cf. Ezekiel 12:3 LXX.
28 Hebrews 4:15.
29 Philippians 2:6–11.
30 See Romans 8:32.

the sake of our salvation from our sins and our iniquities; and He humbled Himself for our sakes, and healed us by His pains.[31] And by the word of His power, He gathered us from the regions of the earth and the whole world, and He became for us a resurrection and salvation from our sins, and taught us that we are members of one another.

3. Therefore, I beseech you, beloved brethren, in the name of our Lord Jesus Christ, that you know well this great dispensation: that God the Word resembled us in everything, except for sin. It is fitting, then, that all rational [beings] know this, being assured of it in their minds[32], and discriminate between good and evil, to be able to become free in His coming to us. For those who have become free and have followed His dispensation, were called His servants. And this calling is not perfection, but righteousness in its time is perfection, and it is what guides to adoption as sons.[33]

And when our Lord Jesus Christ knew that His disciples were about to receive the Spirit of adoption as sons,[34] and that they had known Him and had been taught by the Holy Spirit, He said to them, "No longer do I call you servants … but I have called you friends, for all things that I heard from My Father I have made known to you."[35] For those who have known this in the truth of their intellectual essence, cried out, saying, "For

---

31 See 1 Peter 2:24.
32 Literally: thoughts.
33 "Adoption as sons" is literally "sonship."
34 Ibid.
35 John 15:15.

we have not received the spirit of bondage that we may fear, but the Spirit of adoption as sons[36] by whom we call the Father, 'Our Father.'"[37] So now, Lord, we have learned of what You have bestowed upon us. So if we are children, then heirs—heirs of God, and beloved, and partakers of the inheritance of Christ.[38]

Let these words be clear to you, and he who has not made ready to stand[39] with all his might, let him know that the coming of the Lord [and] Savior will be a condemnation to him. For we are to some people the aroma of death leading to death, and to some the aroma of life leading to life.[40] And this Savior also "is destined for the fall and rising of many in Israel, and for a sign which will be spoken against."[41]

Therefore, I beseech you, beloved brethren, in the name of our Lord Jesus Christ, do not neglect your salvation; rather, let each one rend his heart and not his garments,[42] lest we have put on the monastic garb[43] in vain, thereby preparing for ourselves condemnation. The time has drawn near, and each one will be judged according to his deeds.

And for the obscurity of the words, I wanted to write

---

36 "Adoption as sons" is literally "sonship."
37 Cf. Romans 8:15.
38 See Romans 8:17.
39 That is, to correct himself.
40 See 2 Corinthians 2:16.
41 Luke 2:34.
42 Cf. Joel 2:13.
43 "*Eskeem*" in *Paradise of the Souls*.

further to you, but I have stopped for the sake of the one who said, "Give opportunity to a wise man, and he will become wiser."[44]

I offer you peace in the Lord, [from] your least to the greatest, and the grace of the Lord be with you, beloved brethren, forever. Amen.

---

[44] Cf. Proverbs 9:9.

THE THIRD LETTER

To His Children the Monks, Urging Them to Act Upon the Sayings of the Gospel and the Apostle

1. My children, the rational man, if he prepared to be set free in the day of the coming of our Lord Jesus Christ, would know himself in the essence of the mind. For he who knows himself, knows also the Creator's dispensations in His creatures, who are living in the Lord, and [knows] their partaking in the eternal inheritance, in the fellowship of the saints' membership. Therefore, I beseech you, in the name of our Lord Jesus Christ, to seek what you ought to do unto the Lord, so that He may give all of you the spirit of discernment, that you may discern and know the love I have for you. It is not a bodily love, but spiritual love. And therefore, we have not called you with your bodily names, because they will pass away, but with the firm name, because whoever knows his true name beholds the name of truth, as the name "Jacob" was first when he was [wrestling] with the Angel at night, but when it was

morning his name was called "Israel."[45] "Israel" is translated "the mind that beholds God."

And I know that it is not hidden from you that the enemies of virtue intend to abolish the truth at all time. But at all time, God visits His creation, from the beginning of the world and forever. And those who desire to come to the Creator with all their hearts, He teaches them to worship Him as is right.[46]

And from the severity of weakness, the heaviness of the body, and the warfare of the malicious enemies, the manifest senses of the body have withered, and the senses of the soul have remained powerless, for it does not disintegrate with the body, for its essence[47] is immortal, and neither can it be set free by its [own] righteousness. For this [reason], human beings could not reclaim what is their own, that they may return to their first estate. Therefore, God did for them according to His goodness, and taught them to worship the Father as they ought, because God is Himself One, and the intellectual essence also exists in oneness. Let these words, my beloved, be clear to you: all those gathered [in the communal life], if they were not one heart,[48] would bring wars against themselves[49], and bring judgement upon themselves.

2. So when the Creator looked to the creation, and

---

45 See Genesis 32:28–29.
46 See John 4:24.
47 i.e. the soul's.
48 i.e. living in harmony.
49 *Expanded Paradise* adds: "and issues among themselves".

saw that the blow upon people had enlarged, and that they were in need of physicians to heal them, our Master Jesus Christ, who is their Creator and Healer, sent heralds before Himself. And we are not afraid to say that Moses, who is the arch-prophet and lawgiver, was one of them. And the Spirit who worked in Moses is the same One who worked in all the righteous after him. For they all spoke[50] about the only-begotten Son of God. And John the Baptist was also one of the heralds, "for all the prophets and the law prophesied until John, and from the days of John the Baptist until now the kingdom of heaven suffers violence, and the violent take it by force."[51]

And all those Spirit-mantled knew that none of the Creation was able to heal so great a wound, except for the goodness of the Son, who is the Only-begotten of the Father who sent Him [for the] salvation of the whole world, because He is the great Physician who is able to heal this worsening wound. And the Father, through His goodness, did not spare His Only-begotten, but delivered Him up on behalf of our sins.[52] And for the sake of our salvation from our iniquities, the Only-begotten humbled Himself on our behalf, and by that, He healed all of us. And by the power of His word, He gathered all of us from the whole world, from one end of the earth to the other end, and made for our hearts a resurrection from the earth, and taught us that we are members one of another.

3. Therefore, I beseech you, beloved in the Lord,

---

50 i.e. prophesied.
51 Matthew 11:13,12.
52 See Romans 8:32.

to meditate on what is written, and know that it is the commandments of the Lord. It is a great matter for us that we understand the form which our Lord Jesus Christ took for our sakes, for He resembled us in everything, except for sin.[53] Therefore, we have to become free, so that we may delight in His coming. For through the One who took the form of our foolishness, we became wise, and by His poverty we became rich, and by His weakness we became strong.[54] And He became to all of us a resurrection, and abolished the authority that death had over us. From now on, we have found rest, and do not need another Jesus in the body, because the coming of our Lord Jesus has brought to us a good service,[55] even abolishing all evil, and thereupon He said to His disciples, "No longer do I call you servants, but My brethren."[56] And when they were about to receive the Spirit of adoption as sons,[57] the Holy Spirit taught them to worship the Father as is right.

As for me, the wretched, the bondservant of Jesus Christ, I say that the time wherein we are [living], has brought to us joy, and also mourning and weeping, because many of our race have put on the form of the service of God. Some of them have labored with all their hearts, after they were freed by the coming of Christ, and in these, I delight. And some others have denied the power of godliness, and have labored by the will of their hearts and bodies, so the

---

53 See Hebrews 4:15.
54 See 1 Corinthians 1:24–25.
55 That is, service of God.
56 Cf. John 15:15.
57 "Adoption as sons" is literally "sonship".

coming of the Lord has become a punishment to them, and for these, I mourn. And some too have thought about the length of time and its remoteness, so they weakened their hearts, and cast away from themselves the form of the service of God, and became like beasts; for these too, I weep, because the coming of the Master Christ has become to them a punishment too.

4. As for you, beloved in the Lord, know this time,[58] and be with all your heart an offering to God. I, in truth, my beloved in the Lord, have written to you as he who writes to rational men who could know what is written [in the Scriptures], because I know that whoever knows what is written knows God, and he who knows God, knows His dispensations which He does in His creatures.

Let these words be clear to you, and as I have previously said, I have not written to you with bodily love, but with the spiritual love of God, who is glorified in the counsel of the saints. And know in your hearts, through the one who prays to God for your sakes,[59] that the Lord Christ may send fire into your hearts, which He sent on the earth,[60] so that you may be able to be trained in your resolve and senses, and to discriminate between good and evil, and between the people on the right and left, and the repentant from the unrepentant. And because our Lord knows the tyranny of the devil, He commanded His disciples, saying to them, "Do not lay up for yourselves treasures on earth,"[61] and

---

58 That is, understand the nature of this time.
59 He points to himself.
60 See Luke 12:49.
61 Matthew 6:19.

also said, "Do not worry about tomorrow, for tomorrow will worry about its own things."[62]

I say in truth, my brethren, that when the wind is temperate, all sailors boast, but if there were a change in [the direction of] the wind, then the knowledge of skillful sailors would be made manifest. Likewise, meditate on the time wherein we are [living], how it is. Because of the ambiguity of these words, I have more to say to you, but the one speaking says, "Give opportunity to a wise man, and he will become wiser."[63]

I offer all of you, from the least to the greatest, peace in the Lord, to whom be glory forever. Amen.

---

62 Matthew 6:34.
63 Cf. Proverbs 9:9.

THE FOURTH LETTER

To His Children the Monks; in it He Teaches Them That Servitude to the Law of Virtue is not Servitude but a Sonship of Freedom

1. Anthony writes to his beloved in the Lord, peace.

I do not grow weary from remembering you, O [you] the portion of the Church, and I want you to know that my love for you is not bodily, but is a spiritual love, but the fellowship of the body is not firm nor lasting, but is swayed with strange winds. For everyone who fears God and keeps His commandments, would be a servant of God. And this servitude wherein we are, is not servitude but is righteousness, and it leads to the path of adoption as sons.[64] Therefore, our Lord chose the prophets and apostles, and entrusted them with the apostolic preaching. So they were taken captive by Jesus Christ, because Paul the Apostle says, "I am a prisoner of Jesus Christ, called to

---

64 "Adoption as sons" is literally "sonship."

be an apostle."[65] And the book of the law gave us a good servitude, so that we may be able to have dominion over all the passions, and to complete the good service which is of virtue, about which the apostle spoke. If we come near to grace, then our Lord Jesus Christ says to us, as He said to the disciples, "No longer do I call you servants, but My beloved and My friends, for all things that I heard from My Father I have made known to you."[66]

And those who came near to grace were taught by the Holy Spirit and knew their intellectual essence. So when they knew themselves, they cried out, saying, "For we have not received the spirit of bondage that we may fear, but the Spirit of adoption as sons[67] by whom we cry out, 'O Father, our Father.'"[68] So let us know what God has bestowed upon us, in that He made us sons of His: "If we have become sons, then we are heirs of God, and partakers of the inheritance of the saints."[69]

2. Beloved brethren, co-heirs with the saints, the virtues, all of them, are not far from you, but they are for you and in you. And you are not hidden in this transient world, but are manifest to God. And the Spirit of God does not dwell in the soul or body of a sinner,[70] because He is Holy and far from all guile. And I, in truth, my beloved, write to you as to rational people, who have been able to

---

65 Cf. Ephesians 3:1; Romans 1:1.
66 Cf. John 15:15.
67 "Adoption as sons" is literally "sonship."
68 Cf. Romans 8:15.
69 Cf. Romans 8:17; Colossians 1:12.
70 See Wisdom of Solomon 1:4.

The Fourth Letter

know themselves, because he who has known himself, has known God; therefore, we ought to worship Him as is right.

So now, then, my beloved in the Lord, know yourselves, because those who have known themselves, have known the time,[71] and those who have known their time, were able to remain steadfast, without being troubled by the inconstant words of people. For Arius has risen up in Alexandria, and has mentioned strange words about the only-begotten Son. For Arius has set a beginning for Him who has no beginning, and considered[72] Him to be troubled who is not troubled. And we know that if a person sins against [another] person, for his sake a prayer is offered to God, but he who sins against God, to whom do they direct a prayer for his sake?[73] As to this man, that is Arius, he has brought about against himself a great affair, and has been hit with an incurable blow. For had he known himself truly, his tongue would not have uttered what he had no knowledge of. For it is clear that he did not know himself; therefore, he dared [to speak] about the mystery of the only-begotten Son, to whom with His Father and the Holy Spirit, is due all glory, might, honor, and worship, now and forever. Amen.

---

71 See Romans 13:11.
72 Literally: made.
73 See 1 Samuel 2:25.

THE FIFTH LETTER

To His Children the Monks, Urging Them to Emulate the Saints and to Imitate Their Deeds

1. Anthony writes to his beloved children in the Lord, and offers them peace.

My pure children, the Israelites in their intellectual essence, I do not need to mention your bodily names which pass away with the body, but I call you the true Israelite sons. Know that my love for you is spiritual, and not bodily. Therefore, I do not weary from praying to the Lord for you, that you may know the grace which became yours. For God, through His mercy, rouses all [people] through[74] grace. Therefore, do not lose heart nor slacken, my children, from crying out to the Lord day and night, that you may entreat the goodness of God the Father to grant you help from on high, and [that you may] know what is good for you.

---

74 Literally: by reasons of His.

For in truth, my children, we are dwelling in a den of thieves,[75] and are bound with the bonds of death which is the bearer of us all.[76] Therefore, as of now, do not give sleep to your eyes, nor slumber to your eyelids,[77] that you may raise yourselves [as] sacrifices to the Lord, with all purity, and you may see Him. For without purity, no one is able to see the Lord, as the Apostle says.[78]

And know, my beloved, that if you did good, you would give rest to all the pure saints, because they will not receive the true rest until we are made perfect ourselves. In addition, by your doing good, you give gladness to the angels in their service, and in the coming of the Master Christ. As for me, I the wretched, dwelling in this earthy house, you give joy to my spirit. I know that all of the pure saints, if they see us fall into negligence, are saddened and offer tears and sighs before the Creator, and for the sake of the sighs of the pure, the Lord is angered against the spirits of evil, and He breaks away their evil works from us. But if the saints see in us correction and growth, they are exceedingly gladdened, and continue to offer many prayers for us before the Creator, with gladness and joy, so our Lord rejoices by our good deeds and by the testimonies of His saints and their prayers. And He bestows upon us many gifts. For our Lord is always with His creatures that are carrying out His commandments, as we have already said in our letters.

---

75 Literally: house of thieves.
76 That is, we are bound by its power.
77 See Psalm 132:4.
78 See Hebrews 12:14.

2. Let us weep now, my children, before His goodness, and say as the Psalm said, "What shall we give for the benefits which He rendered to us?"[79] And let us also say with David the Psalmist, "What profit is there in my blood, if I go down to perdition?"[80] I want you to know then what I am saying to you and testifying about.

Truly, my children, whoever does not hate what concerns the material, earthly nature, and all its works, with all his heart, and does not extend his mind on high, to the Father of all—he cannot be saved. As for the one who does so, our Lord will have compassion on his labors, and will grant him the invisible, immaterial fire, that it may burn all the passions within him and purify his mind. Then the Spirit of our Lord Jesus Christ will dwell in him, and be with him, so that he may be able to worship the Father as is right. So if we remain reconciled with this material nature, then we are enemies of God, His angels, and all His saints.

3. And I beseech you in the name of our Lord Jesus Christ, that you should not neglect your life and salvation, and should not let this transient, fleeting time steal from you the eternal time which is everlasting; nor [let] this fleshly body take you away from the kingdom of light which is immeasurable and ineffable; nor [let] this passing, perishing throne bring you down from the thrones of the company of the angels.

Truly, my children, my soul is baffled and my spirit is

---

79 Cf. Psalms 115:3 LXX.
80 Cf. Psalms 29:10 LXX.

distracted, because all of us have been given the freedom of choice, to do the works of the saints, but we are intoxicated by the passions, like people drunk with the pleasure of wine, and we have not desired to lift up our minds to seek the heavenly glory, and have not imitated the works of all the saints, and have not gone after their footsteps, that we may inherit the eternal glory with them.

4. And know, my beloved, that the powers—which are holy, high, rational, and luminous—and the perceivable natures, are all created for one thing—that is, the glorification of God: the angels, archangels, thrones, dominions, cherubim, seraphim, sun, moon, and stars; the patriarchs, the prophets, and the apostles; the demons, devils, spirits of malice, and rulers of the air. All these belong to the ingenuity of the Holy Trinity: The Father and the Son and the Holy Spirit. Some of them, for the sake of their perceptible motion, God named according to their works. And those whose growth increased, were glorified more abundantly by God, to whom is the glory, the power, and the honor, with His good Father and the Holy Spirit,[81] forever and ever. Amen.

---

81 *Expanded Paradise* adds here: "from us all."

THE SIXTH LETTER

To His Children the Monks Dwelling in Arsinoe; Informing Them of the Demons' Warfare and the Help of the Holy Powers, and Urging Them to be Patient and to Bring to Completion That for Which They Have Gone Out

1. Anthony offers peace to his beloved children dwelling in Arsinoe and its surrounding regions, and to all who are with them, and to all who draw near to the Lord with all their hearts. Peace to you all, from your least to your greatest, whether man or woman,[82] who are Israelites in truth.

You have received the happy blessedness by the coming of grace upon[83] you. But you must not be negligent in the war for the sake of the One who has visited you, shining from on high, so that you may become unto Him a pure,

---

82 This indicates that there were nuns—that is, virgins—under the guidance of Abba Anthony. [Footnote is retrieved from *Expanded Paradise*].
83 Literally: in.

holy sacrifice. For we know how this nature, which is of the essence, fell from its height to the bottom of disgrace and humiliation, and how the merciful God visited it by His law through the hands of Moses and the prophets, and at last this was [done] by His only-begotten Son, who is our great Archbishop and our true Physician, who is able to heal us of our passions[84]. So He took our body, and gave Himself up for us and for our sins. Because of our foolishness, He took the form of foolishness; and because of our weakness, He took the form of weakness; and because of our poverty, He took the form of poverty; and because of our death, He tasted death. All of these He endured for our sake, and by His death He saved us.

2. Therefore we have to struggle with whatever the struggle demands, so that by us all the saints may be gladdened, who pray for us at the time of our negligence, so the one who sows and the one who reaps may rejoice together. And you should know, my children, the great suffering I am in because of you. For I look at the labors of the saints for you, and their sighs, and their prayers which they offer for your sakes at all time before God. Therefore, be diligent to imitate them, for they have considered the dispensations of their Creator, in His wondrous incarnation and His labors for our salvation. And they have also considered the foolishness of the enemy who seeks at all time our destruction in hell, which is his portion with his armies, because they always seek to destroy us with this great destruction.

---

84 Or: pains.

Therefore, I beseech you, my beloved children, to understand this, and look into the dispensations of our Creator and His visitation for us, through the manifest and hidden preaching. But though we, who are called, were rational, we have become as irrational, because of our inclination to the will of the enemy and the evil-doer and the father of lying. And I want you to know how many are the multitudes of angels and how many are the multitudes of the plots of the devils and their countless variety; and they, when they learned that we have become aware of our passions and disgrace, and that we have become diligent in escaping from their bad deeds working in us, and not only that, but we do not listen to their evil counsels which they sow into us—they undertook their works despite many of us who were laughing at them. And they know that the gift of their Creator has become death to them here, and they have been prepared to be an inheritance of hell, because of their negligence and abundant malice.

3. And for the sake of this, my beloved children, I do not weary from praying for you night and day, that the Lord may open the eyes of your hearts, to see [how] greatly abundant is the devils' cunning, and their evil which they bring upon us every day; and that He may give you a watchful heart and a spirit of discernment, to be able to lift yourselves up [as] a pure, living sacrifice for God; and that you may be on your guard against the devils' envy of you at all times, all their evil counsels, their opposing warfare against us in secret, their concealed evil, their misleading spirits, their blasphemous thoughts, lack of faithfulness and wandering of heart which they sow within us at all

The Sixth Letter

times, their subtle disturbances which they bring every day with sorrow of heart, their anger, and their slander which they sow in us, that we may slander one against another, justify ourselves alone and judge others, curse each other, speak sweetly with the tongue while bitterness is in our hearts, judge others for their manifest deeds while the thief is inside us, and fight and resist each other so that we make our word stand and appear honorable. They also urge us to [do] other deeds which are beyond our strength, and weaken us in the matters that are for our benefit, so they make us laugh at the time of weeping, and weep at the time of joy, intending to lead us astray from the upright path, to enslave us through their tyranny.

And I do not have time now to speak about the rest of their evils, one by one, save that I would say that if our hearts were filled with such evils, becoming to us like food, then evil would grow worse in us and would become rooted; and an evil punishment will be ours. Therefore, we should not grow weary of entreating the goodness of the Father, that His help may come and support us in all our works, because there are numerous evils that lead to perdition, because this vessel[85] wherein we live is nothing but a house filled with war.

4. And I say to you, my children, that every man who takes delight in his thoughts falls by his will, because he finds joy in what is sown into him of these things, and he thinks that they are great mysteries. And he justifies himself alone with what he does, and is a dwelling for the

---

85   i.e. the body.

evil spirit who counsels him to evil, his body becoming filled with his vile, hidden mysteries. So the one who is like this, the passions of the demons reign in him, because he has not cast them away from him.

Therefore, we ought to know the snares of the devil and his schemes, and turn aside and run away from them, because the iniquities and sins which are from the demons are not manifest nor bodily, for they do not have bodies which can be seen, but we become bodies for them when our souls accept thoughts of darkness from them. And when they [the thoughts] are accepted from them, they [the demons] make them manifest in the body.

Therefore, take heed, my children, that you do not let there be a place for them in you, lest the anger of the Lord comes upon us, so they rejoice and laugh at us, then depart from us. Do not cast my words away from you, for they know that our life is from one another. For who has seen God since the world began, that he may take hold of Him lest He goes away from him, and that he may rejoice in Him, and He may save him from the opposition of this burdensome body? Or who has seen the devil bodily standing before him, so that he may run away from him? The devils, however, are present in secret, and we make them manifest through our works. And all of them are one intellectual essence, but when they went far from God, different names were given them, because of their diverse works, and their multitude [of names] was firmly set on them for their multitude of evils. And these names are: devils, Satan,[86] demons, evil spirits, unclean [spirits], apostates, rulers of this world of darkness, and many other names like these.

5. As for the heavenly powers, their names are: archangels,[87] angels, thrones, dominions, authorities, cherubim, seraphim, and so on. These names were firmly set for them because they kept the will of their Creator. As for those who hated the burdensomeness of this body which we are clothed in, and who cast it away from them, some of them were called patriarchs, others prophets, kings, priests, judges, and apostles. These names became theirs, whether they were men or women, because of their various deeds and their inclination to goodness, and many other reasons like these. Nevertheless, they are all of one principle and one essence. Therefore, whoever sins against his neighbor, sins against himself, and whoever does evil to his neighbor, does it to his own self.

For who could weary the Lord, or give Him rest, or serve Him as he ought [to serve], or praise Him as He ought to be [praised], or honor Him as befits His honor, or exalt Him as is meet for Him? For this is beyond our ability because of the burdensomeness of the passions of this body upon us. So it is necessary, when we have learned this, that we rouse up God who is dwelling in us, through our deeds, our gladness, and our compassion toward each other. And we should not love ourselves only, so that we may not become of the portion of the evil [one].

---

86   Literally: Satans.
87   Literally: archs or chiefs.

But we should know ourselves, because he who has known himself, has known all the creatures which God made out of nothing into existence, and has also known the enduring intellectual nature which is hidden in this dissolving body, that its [the intellectual nature's] deeds may be seen in it [the body] and through it. And he who knew this, was able to love God alone, and he who loves the Lord, loves all.

6. Therefore, my beloved children, do not cease nor be wearied of loving one other, but make this body, with which you are clothed, a censer in which you raise all your thoughts and evil councils, and place them before the Lord, by raising your hearts to Him—that is, to the creative[88] Mind—and beseech Him with all the might of the mind that He may be gracious unto you, by the coming of His immaterial fire from on high to you, to consume all that is in this censer and purge it. So the contrary priests of Baal would be afraid, and run away from before you, as they ran away before Elijah the prophet.[89] And then you would see a trace of a man bringing up water from the divine fountain, and giving you[90] the spiritual rain, which is of the Spirit, the Paraclete. Therefore, my children, if you have received these virtuous gifts, do not think that they are of your works, but it is a holy power taking part with you in all your works.

And I beseech you to be diligent and continue in your

---

88 "Creative" here meaning the capacity to cause something that did not exist to exist.

89 See 1 Kings 18:38–40.

90 Literally: raining for you.

The Sixth Letter

good works, so that all the saints and my spirit, I the poor, may rejoice in you, for we are all created of one principle and one invisible intellectual essence. For the one who knows himself, learns that he is an immortal essence, and that our Lord Jesus Christ is the true Mind[91] of the Father, of whom is the realization of all the rational nature which was created in the likeness of His Image. For He is the Head of the body and the Head of the Church as Paul the Apostle says.[92] And therefore we are all members of one another, and are one body of Christ.[93] "The head cannot say to the feet, 'I have no need of you,' but if one member suffers, all the members suffer with it,"[94] as the Apostle also said.

But if any member becomes estranged from the body and loses his connection with the head, because he takes delight in the passions of his flesh, this means that his wound is incurable, and that he no longer remembers his beginning nor his end. Therefore, the Father of the creation is moved with compassion over our wound which cannot be cured by any of the creatures, except by the goodness of the Father alone; so He sent to us His Only-begotten, who, because of our servitude, took the form of a servant and gave Himself up for the sake of our sins.

7. My beloved children in the Lord, the pure Israelite sons, be ready to go to the Lord, to offer yourselves to God [as] pure sacrifices, this which no one may acquire

---

91 Or: Intellect.
92 See Colossians 1:18.
93 See 1 Corinthians 12:27.
94 See 1 Corinthians 12: 21,26

without purification[95]. Do you not know, my beloved, that the enemies of virtue plot evil against the truth? Therefore, also, beware and give no sleep to your eyes, nor slumber to your eyelids,[96] and cry out to your Creator day and night, that help may come to you from on high, and may keep your hearts and thoughts in Christ. And I tell you in truth, my beloved, that our negligence and humiliation and deviation from the way are not loss to us only, but they are wearisome to the angels and all the saints in Christ Jesus.

Truly, my children, our humiliation causes all of them sorrow, but our salvation and glory cause them joy and rejoicing. And know that the loving-kindness of the Father has not ceased for a moment since His first motion until today, from doing good to us, so that we may not draw our death to us by the misuse of our free will which He created for us. Therefore, we should all the more keep the love toward each other, because he who loves his brother, loves God,[97] and he who loves God, loves himself, as John the Apostle says.

8. And I beseech you, my beloved children, that you may also know that we were created [as] ones who have control over ourselves,[98] and therefore the spirits of deception, which surround us, stand against us. But know what is written in the Psalm: "The angel of the Lord encamps around those who fear Him, and saves them out

---

95 Or: refining.
96 Psalms 132:4.
97 See 1 John 4:21.
98 "over our wills" in the *Paradise of the Soul*.

The Sixth Letter

of all their sorrows."⁹⁹

And I also want you to know that all those who have gone away from virtue, in them the deceit of the devils is perfected, and what is written is fulfilled in them, that they are sons of Satan. For the devil fell down from his first heavenly rank because of his pride, and has become always desirous of making all who have drawn near to the Lord with all their hearts, fall into this characteristic into which he fell—that is, pride[100] and the love of vainglory. And with these, and others, the devils began to war against us, thinking of separating us from God. And because they also know that he who loves his brother, loves God, for by reason of their enmity toward virtue, and their madness, they sow in our hearts [thoughts] that we may hate one another, making one of us not even desirous of seeing his brother or saying a single word to him.

Therefore, my children, I inform you that many have truly labored in virtue to the uttermost, but by their lack of discernment, they have killed themselves. And I know that this is nothing to wonder at, for if you become idle, [ceasing] from work, because of your mastery of the virtues in yourselves, you will fall into this demonic sickness, which is the lack of discernment, and you will think that you have drawn near to God, and that your life is in the light, while you are truly in darkness.

9. What need did our Lord Jesus Christ have that He girded Himself with a towel and laid aside His garment

---

99 Cf. Psalms 34:7.
100 Literally: grandeur.

and poured water into a basin and washed the feet of His inferiors,[101] except to teach us humility, and show it to us with this example which He did? All those who want to return to their first estate, will not be able to except by humility, because from the beginning the motion of pride is what made its owner fall from heaven. So if there were not in man deep[102] humility, with all the heart, all the intention, all the spirit, all the soul, and all the body, he would not inherit the kingdom of God, as it is written.[103]

Truly, my beloved children in the Lord, I beseech my Creator night and day, in whose hand is my spirit, that He may enlighten the eyes of your hearts, that you may know first my love for you, and after that you may see your disgrace and know it, because he who knows his disgrace is the one who seeks the true, elect glory, because he who has known his death, has known his eternal life.

10. And I fear for you, my children, lest [spiritual] famine and poverty overtake you in the road leading to the place in which you can gain wealth. And I desire to see you here in the body, but I would rather await that age in which there is no grief, sorrow, nor groaning, but gladness and joy to all who are worthy of it, and that we may meet there soon, and I see you.

And what is more, I have much to say to you, but this is not its time, but it is time for me to offer each one by name, my beloved children, peace in the Lord, to whom belongs praise now and forever and ever. Amen.

---

101 See John 13:4–5.

102 Literally: much.

103 See 1 Corinthians 6:10; Galatians 5:21; Ephesians 5:5.

THE SEVENTH LETTER

To His Children the Monks, in Which He Informs Them That Our Salvation is Not Through an Angel, Nor Through a Man, but Through God, the Incarnate Word; And He Urges Them to Struggle with What the Struggle Demands, to Receive Salvation

1. I know the grace of our Lord Jesus Christ, that though He was rich, yet for our sakes He became poor, that we through His poverty might become rich,[104] that we might be set free through His submission, and strengthened through His weakness, and become wise through the One thought foolish, and rise through His death, and cry out with the Apostle, saying, "Though we have known Christ in the flesh, yet now we know Him thus no longer."[105]

In truth, my beloved, I say to you that these words are subtle in their meaning, and I have many things to

---

104 See 2 Corinthians 8:9.
105 Cf. 2 Corinthians 5:16.

say on it, but this is not the time for their explanation. Rather I begin, and offer you peace in the Lord, my blessed children, and inform you that we who want to draw near to our Creator must struggle for the sake of the salvation of our souls from the passions [in accordance with] the intellectual law. For because of the worsening of deceit, the delight of the passions, and the multitude of demonic temptations, our perception has weakened and the motions of our souls have died. And therefore, we were not able to know the value[106] of our intellectual essence, because of the passions we had fallen into. And we have no salvation except through our Lord Jesus Christ,[107] for Paul the Apostle wrote saying that by the first Adam was death, and by Christ was life.[108] Thus, the Master Christ our Lord is the Life of all rational [beings] who are created according to the likeness of His Image, which is the true Mind of the Father. As for the Image of the Father, It is invariable and unchangeable, but the manifest image in His creatures is variable [and changeable], in which, therefore, came our death, and it is at odds with the intellectual nature, and from it we were born with a body, and became a home filled with war.

And I testify to you and say that all the virtues were destroyed in us, and when God the Father looked to our weakness, and that we could not endure His appearance in us as His form is in truth[109], He sent His only-begotten

---

106 Or: measure.

107 See Acts 4:12.

108 See 1 Corinthians 15:22.

109 *Paradise of the Soul* adds "and justice."

Son, and He took our body and visited His creatures, servants, and saints with His gifts.

2. Therefore, my beloved children, I beseech you through my love for you, that you draw near to the Lord with all your hearts and souls, and that you may know that all the works we offer the Lord by the grace which He gave us, cannot be proportional to His humbling Himself for us. For He is in no need of us, and neither did He come to us for the sake of our humility, but out of the greatness of His goodness and mercy, and out of His unfathomable love, He did not deal with us according to our sins, but He made the moon and the stars for the service of this dark house, that is, the world, for the sake of raising up the body. And He made many hidden things serve us, things which we do not see with our bodily eyes. As for us, because of the multitude of our sins, we made their service for us vain.

What shall we say in the day of judgement to our Lord? For what goodness has He not done for us, by Himself? For the patriarchs did not labor for our sakes, nor did the priests teach us, nor did the rulers and kings fight for us, nor were the apostles persecuted for our sakes; rather, the beloved Son the Word died on behalf of us all. Therefore, we should make ready with all purity, and with it should train our senses which are variable between good and evil. For we all have to pass and meet our Lord Jesus who came to us and saved us by all His dispensations, and who became like us in everything, except for sin [alone]. And all this, to some people, is foolishness, because of the multitude of the evil of the malicious devils, which is in them; and to [other] people a doubt,[110] and as to others a benefit, to [yet] others wisdom and power, and to others resurrection and life.

3. My children, let this be clear to you, that the coming of our Lord became a condemnation to those, and life to these. But about these, Jeremiah the prophet says, "The days are coming, when I will put my law in their minds, and write it on their hearts; and I will be their God, and they shall be My people. No more shall every man teach the people of his city, nor his brother, saying to him, 'Know the Lord,' for they all shall know Me, from the least of them to the greatest of them. And I will refine them from their iniquities, and I will also remember their sins no more."[111] But about those, the Apostle says: "That every mouth may be stopped, and all the world may become subject unto God,"[112] "because, although they knew God, they did not glorify Him as God,"[113] for lack of their knowledge, which could not accept the wisdom of God; therefore, wrath will come upon them.

And now, my children, I see that each one of us has delivered himself by his will to evils. And these have been made perfect in us, and have reigned over us, because of our foolishness. Therefore, our Lord took the form of our foolishness, that He may save us by it, and fulfilled all His dispensations [even] to the death of the cross, that

---

110 See 1 Corinthians 1:23.
111 Cf. Jeremiah 31:31–34.
112 Cf. Romans 3:19.
113 Romans 1:21.

through His death and resurrection there may be for us an excellent[114] resurrection, and the power of death, which is the power of the devil, may be abolished. And if we liberate ourselves and imitate His humility, we become His disciples.

4. In truth, my beloved children in the Lord, I say to you that I am extremely troubled in my body and spirit, for we have been given the names of saints, and have put on their garment and boast of this before the unbelieving, all the while we do not have the power of labor as the saints, and I am afraid that the saying of the Apostle may be fulfilled in us: "Having the form of godliness, but denying its power."[115] For the sake of my love for you, I do not cease to pray to God on your behalf, that you may understand your life which is hidden in you, and may know by what [thing] you are worthy to inherit that which is not seen. And know, my beloved, that if we completed our works with all our might, according to His will, this would be our duty, for it is natural to our essence, and in that we have no merit, for everyone who serves God and seeks Him with all his heart, does that with his natural essence. So if a sin comes from him, he is blamed for it, it being foreign to his natural essence.

Therefore, understand this, and know that I have not concealed from you anything, which I have not taught you, of that which is for your salvation. And I inform you too that the flesh is opposed to the Spirit, as Paul the

---

114 Literally: virtuous.
115 2 Timothy 3:5.

Apostle said.[116] For those who want to conduct themselves through the way of asceticism in Christ Jesus, should cast out of themselves carnal lusts, by praying to the Lord Jesus Christ. And He, through His mercy and compassion, will destroy from them the hardships and temptations, which come upon them concerning the body, as came upon our fathers the Apostles. And those, by their patience, destroyed the power of the enemy, which is idolatry, and our Lord gave them comfort and power, by saying to them, "In the world you will have tribulation, but be strong, I have overcome the world."[117] And He also said to them, "If they persecuted the prophets and persecuted Me, they will persecute you also, and if they hated Me, they will hate you also."[118] But be strong, and know that, by your patience, you destroy the power of the enemy.

And I too, my blessed children, want you to keep this saying, and also what Paul the Apostle said, "For I consider that the sufferings of this present time are not worthy to be compared with the glory which shall be revealed in us."[119] And know that, because of my love for you, I have spoken to you these few, spiritual words, that I may comfort your hearts, because I know that if the mind were roused, it would not need a multitude of words. And I rejoice in the Lord for your sakes, my beloved children, who are pure in your intellectual essence. And I want you to know the greatness of the gifts which have become ours from the

---

116 See Galatians 5:17.
117 Cf. John 16:33.
118 Cf. John 15:20,18.
119 Romans 8:18.

Lord, for our preservation and growth, and that you may hold on to the natural works related to the essence, [and] not to the works that are not related to the essence.

5. I, the wretched, inform you also that our Lord has roused my mind from the sleep of death, by His grace. And mourning and weeping have become mine in what remains for me of this fleeting time on earth, because I think about what we shall give the Lord in place of what He has done unto us![120] For He made His angels serve us, His prophets prophesy unto us, and His Apostles preach to us, and what is greater than all this: He sent forth His only-begotten Son for our salvation.

Therefore, I beseech you to rouse your hearts by the fear of the Lord, and know that John the forerunner baptized with water for repentance, that he may draw us to the baptism of our Lord Jesus who baptized us with the Holy Spirit and fire, which is the fire of good works. So let us make ready now by purifying ourselves, body and spirit, that we may accept the baptism of our Lord Jesus Christ and do [good works], and lift ourselves as an acceptable offering to Him, because the Spirit of Comfort whom we received in Baptism gives us the work of repentance, to restore us to our first estate, that we may become heirs of the inheritance that does not pass away.

And know also that all those who are baptized into Christ have put on Christ, as Paul the Apostle said,[121] and they receive the grace of the Holy Spirit. For neither slave

---

120 See Psalms 116:12.
121 See Galatians 3:27.

nor free, neither male nor female, may receive this grace except [that] these earthly[122] languages [i.e. names] are put away from him, and he accepts the teaching of the Holy Spirit, in whom he will receive the eternal inheritance of the kingdom of heaven and the worshiping of the Father as is right, in spirit and truth.

6. Let no one of you, my children, say that there is no condemnation to us on the day of the second[123] coming of our Lord, but let him know that the first coming of our Master Christ has become to us a condemnation truly on that day if we do not fulfill His statutes. And know that all those Spirit-mantled pray at all time on our behalf, that we may unite to our Lord, and inherit what is prepared for us since the beginning, and put on once again our first image, which is of the essence, of which we were stripped by the transgression. For the Image of the Father [which is] continually in the Spirit-mantled reveals to them His goodness, and reminds them of that which is written and says, "Comfort, yes, comfort My people, O priests, and speak in the heart of Jerusalem."

And I ask the God of peace at all time—in whose mercy He visits His creatures and reveals His goodness in them—that He may give you wisdom, knowledge, grace, and a spirit of discernment, that you may understand what I have written to you of the commandments of the Lord, and to do them, that they may keep you pure to the last breath. And He accepts from me my entreaty which I offer Him for the salvation of you all, my beloved children in

---

122 Literally: bodily or carnal.
123 Literally: last.

the Lord, to whom is the glory, majesty, and honor, forever and ever. Amen.

www.ingramcontent.com/pod-product-compliance
Lightning Source LLC
Chambersburg PA
CBHW031435040426
42444CB00006B/829